Garfield
A TO Z ZOO

Created by Jim Davis
Illustrated by Mike Fentz and Dave Kühn

Random House  New York

Copyright © 1984 by United Feature Syndicate, Inc. All rights reserved under International and Pan-American Copyright Conventions. Published in the United States by Random House, Inc., New York, and simultaneously in Canada by Random House of Canada Limited, Toronto.

Library of Congress Cataloging in Publication Data: Davis, Jim. Garfield A to Z zoo.
SUMMARY: While unconscious after a bump on the head, Garfield the cat dreams of fantastic zoo animals with names beginning with each letter of the alphabet.
[1. Animals—Fiction. 2. Cats—Fiction. 3. Alphabet] I. Fentz, Mike, ill. II. Kühn, Dave, ill. III. Title.
PZ7.D2924Gaq 1984 [E] 83-17697 ISBN: 0-394-86483-2
Manufactured in the United States of America 234567890

One day Garfield decided to walk to the zoo to find animals starting with all the letters of the alphabet.

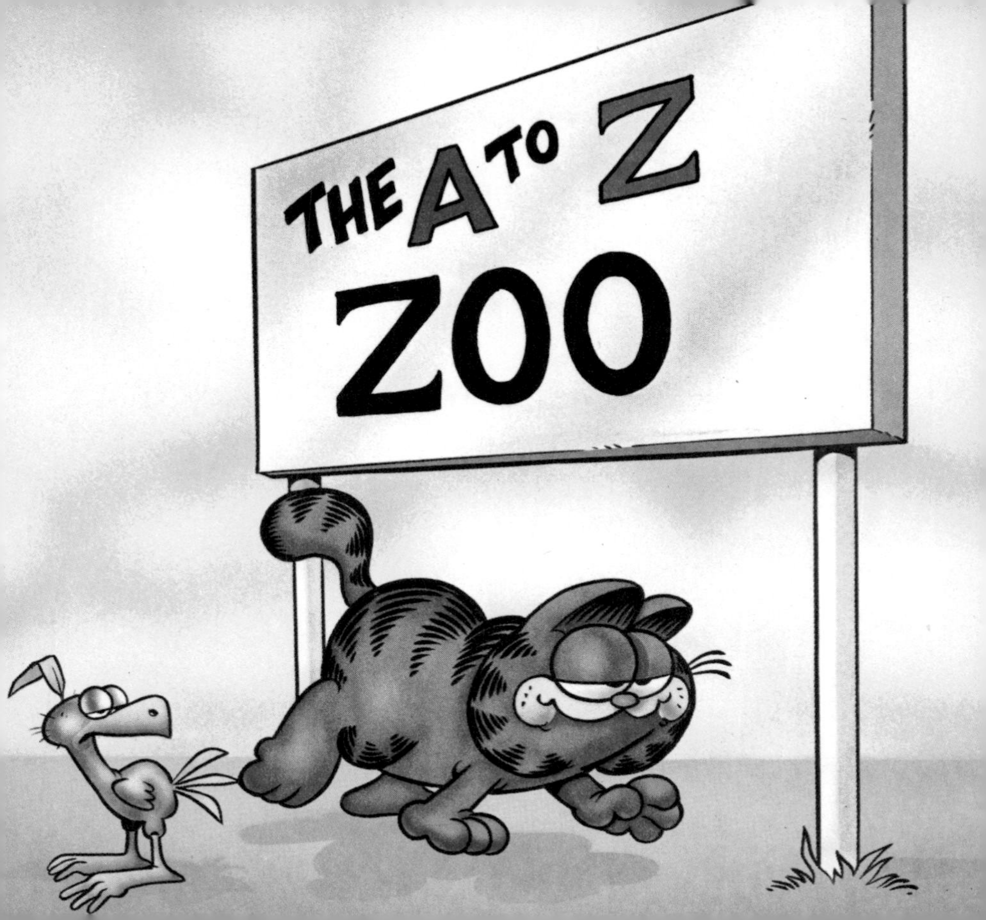
THE A TO Z
ZOO

A friendly Grak Bird paused to say hi in Grak talk.

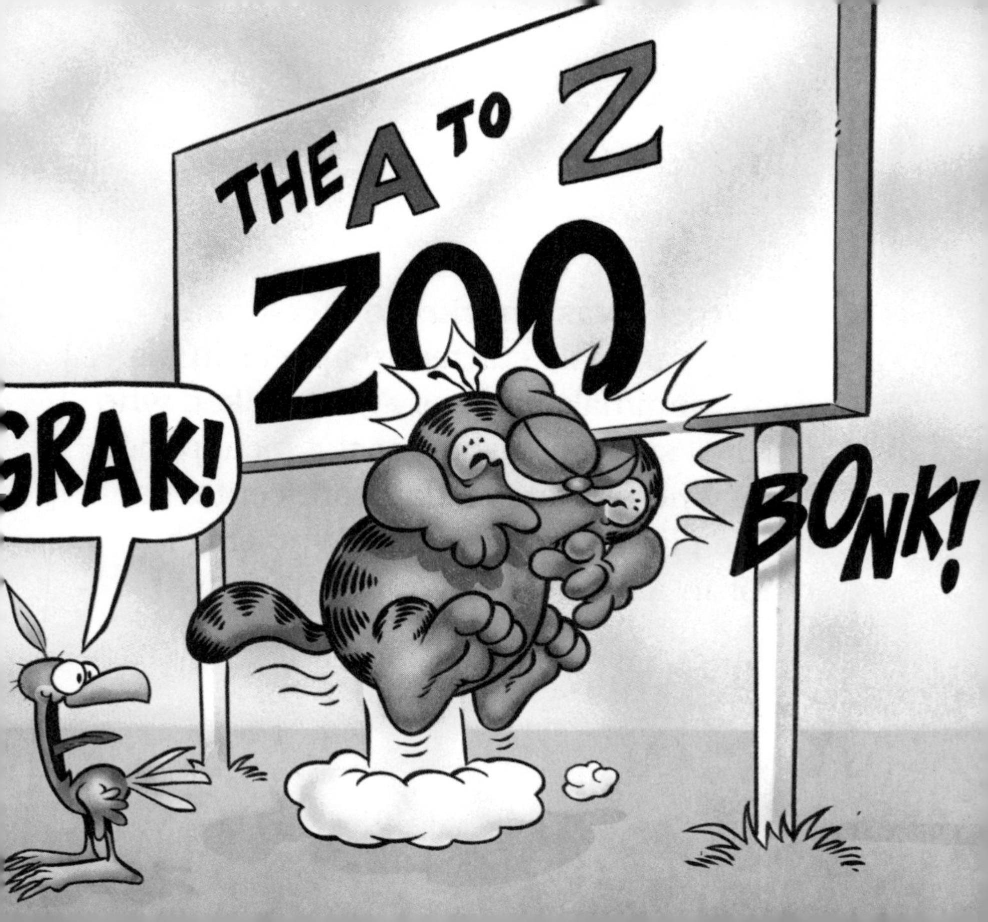
THE A TO Z
ZOO
GRAK!
BONK!

Garfield was knocked out cold, and strange animals started to appear in his mind...animals such as Aquawalker, who teaches swamp surfing at the local pond; Bob, who operates a day-care center for house plants; Caterwauler, who sings tenor in a barbershop quartet;

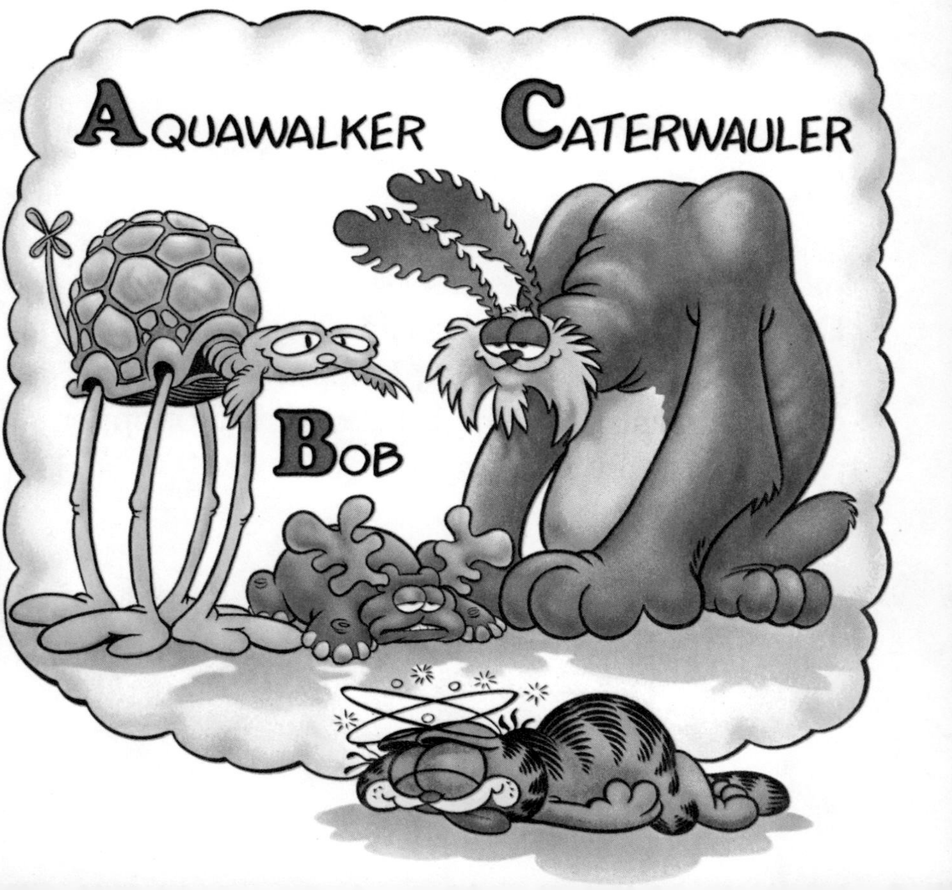
AQUAWALKER
CATERWAULER
BOB

Duckbilled Dapple, who is a Ping-Pong instructor at the YMCA; Enock, who is a gold medalist in the high hurdles; Flaphopper, who is actually a bug;

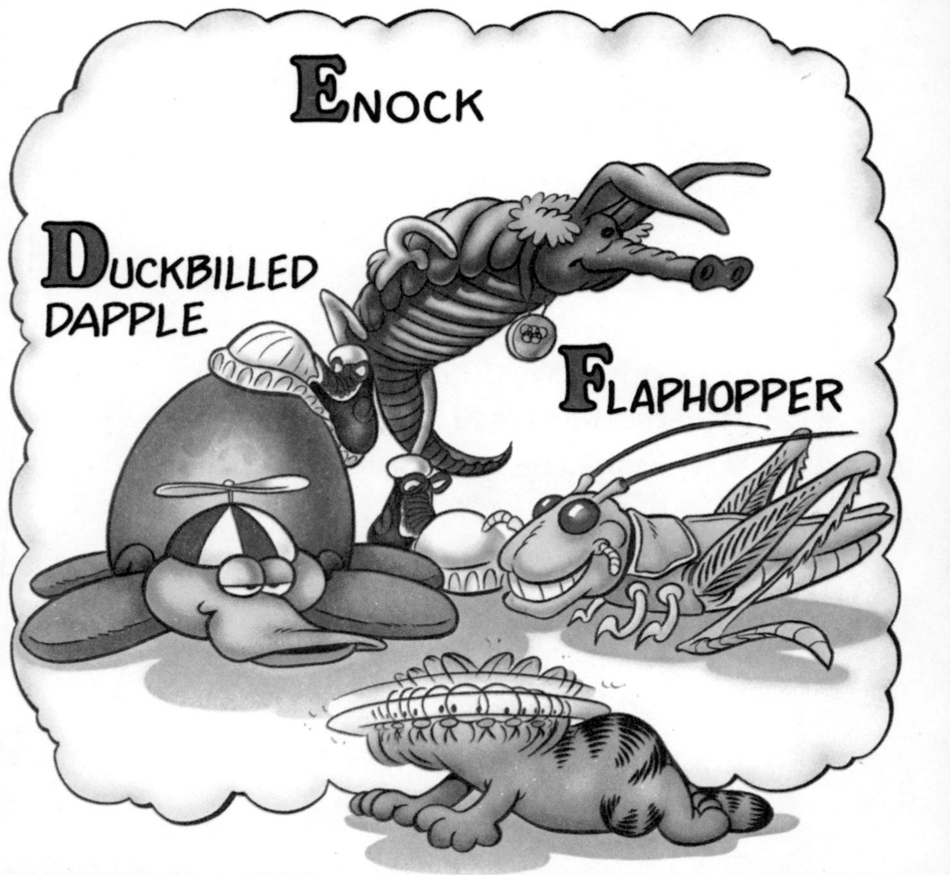
ENOCK
DUCKBILLED DAPPLE
FLAPHOPPER

Gordonus, who does great bird impersonations; Hoppo, who plays "Go Fish"; Ig, who is a plant lover;

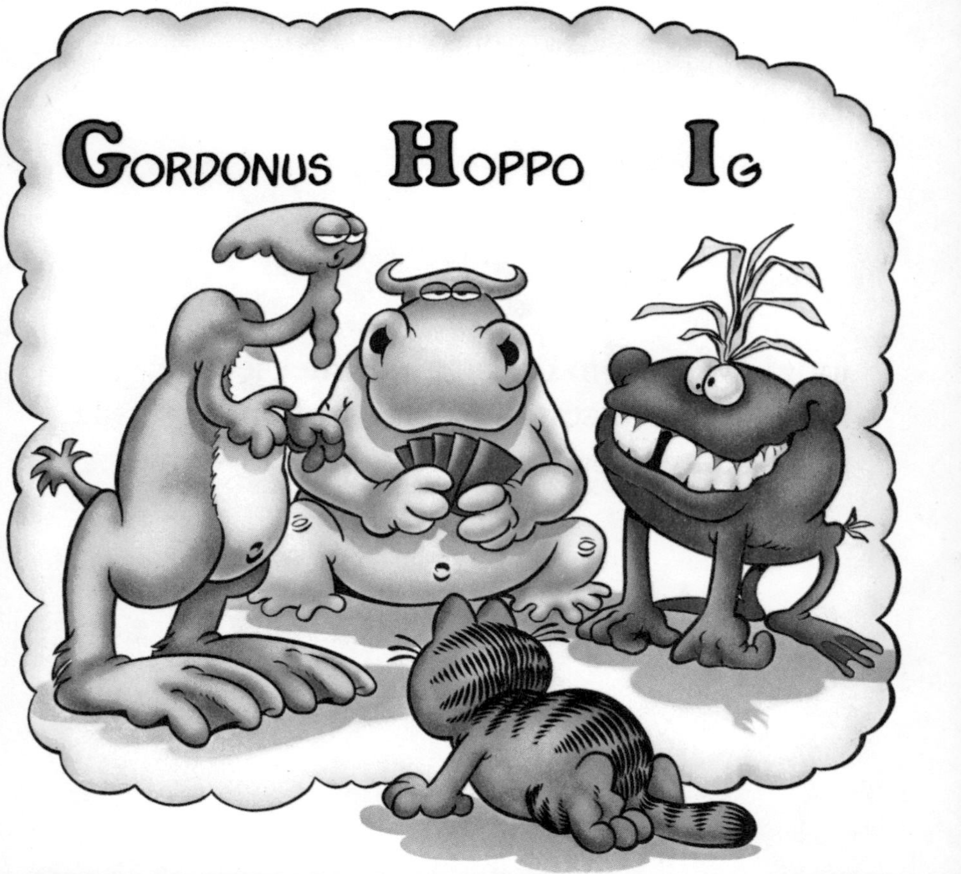
GORDONUS
HOPPO
IG

Junglewart, who doesn't like cheesecake;
Kak, who is a state-fair blue-ribbon hog caller;
Lelander, whose hobby is baking brownies;

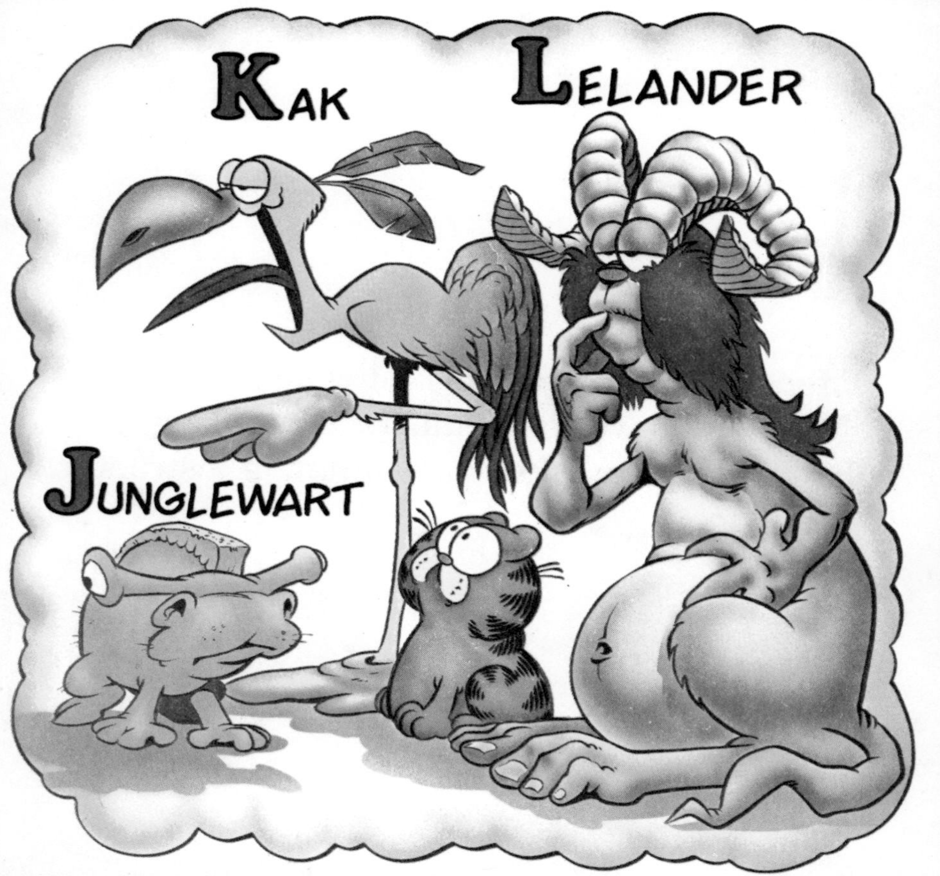
KAK
LELANDER
JUNGLEWART

Mongo, who is a janitor at the aquarium;
Nibitz, who works summers as a fishing
bobber; Opkar, who is a swimming instructor;

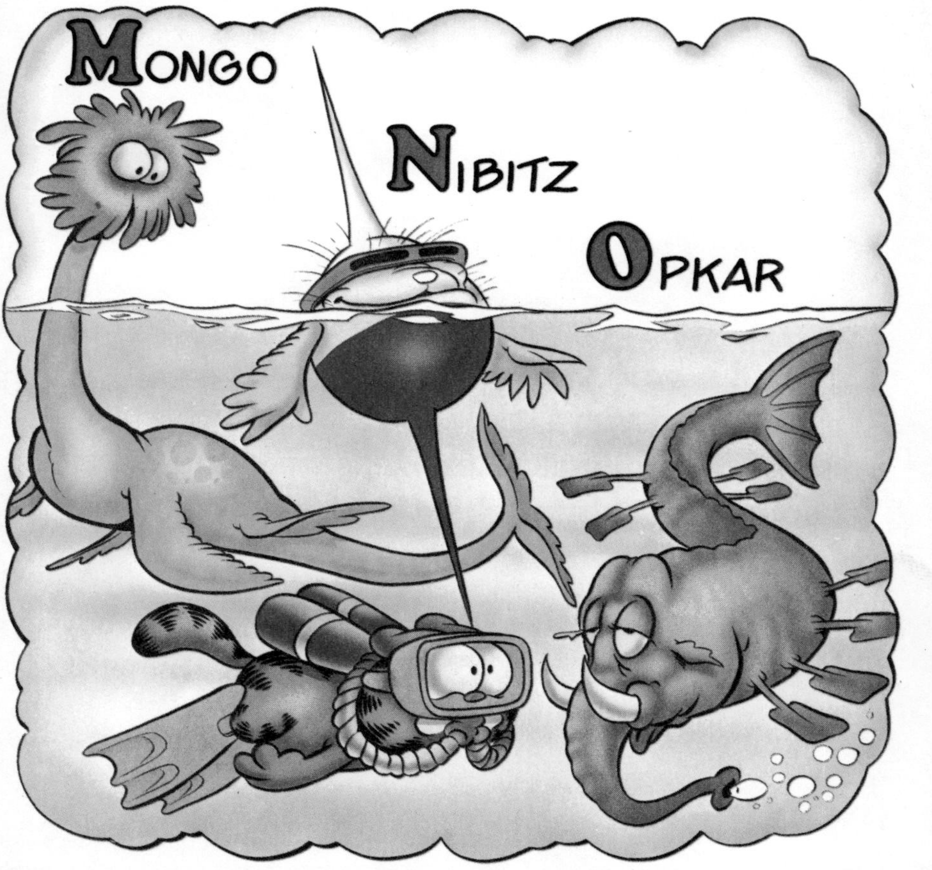
MONGO
NIBITZ
OPKAR

Paladis, who personally knows the Loch Ness Monster; Quid, who plays a great game of handball; Rex Imperius, who once skippered a shrimp boat on Lake Michigan;

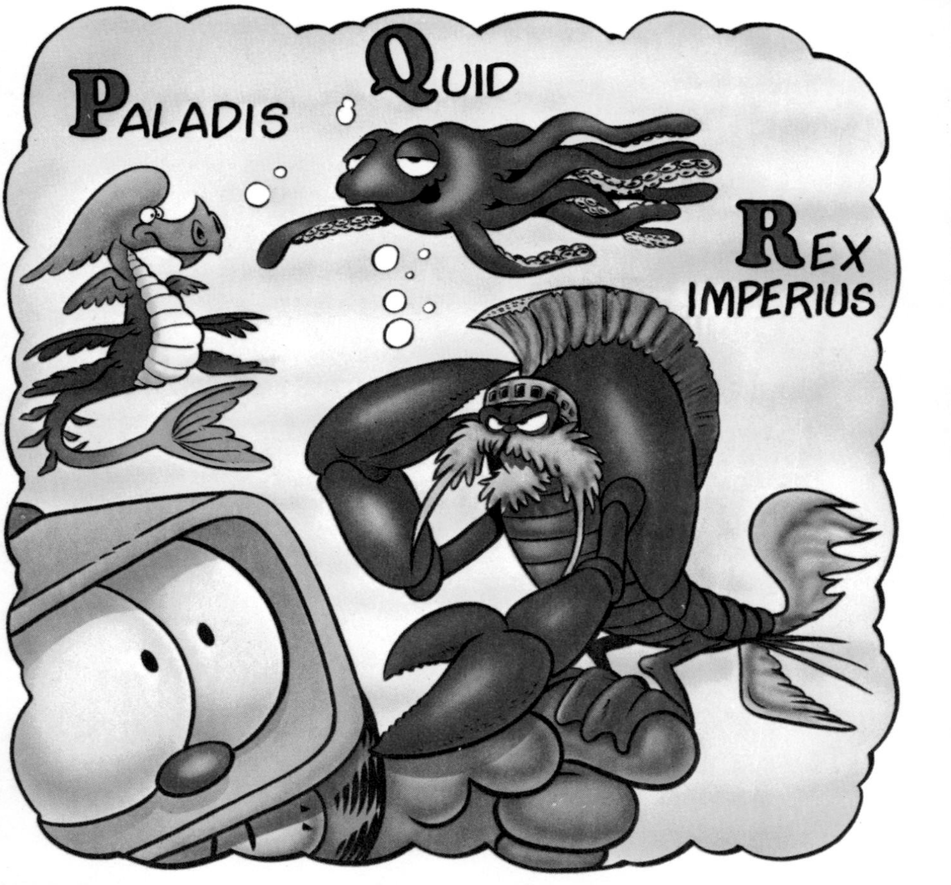
PALADIS
QUID
REX
IMPERIUS

Spaldergoth, whose nickname is Blinky;
Tragoon, who collects leaves; Ugal, who is
his own best friend;

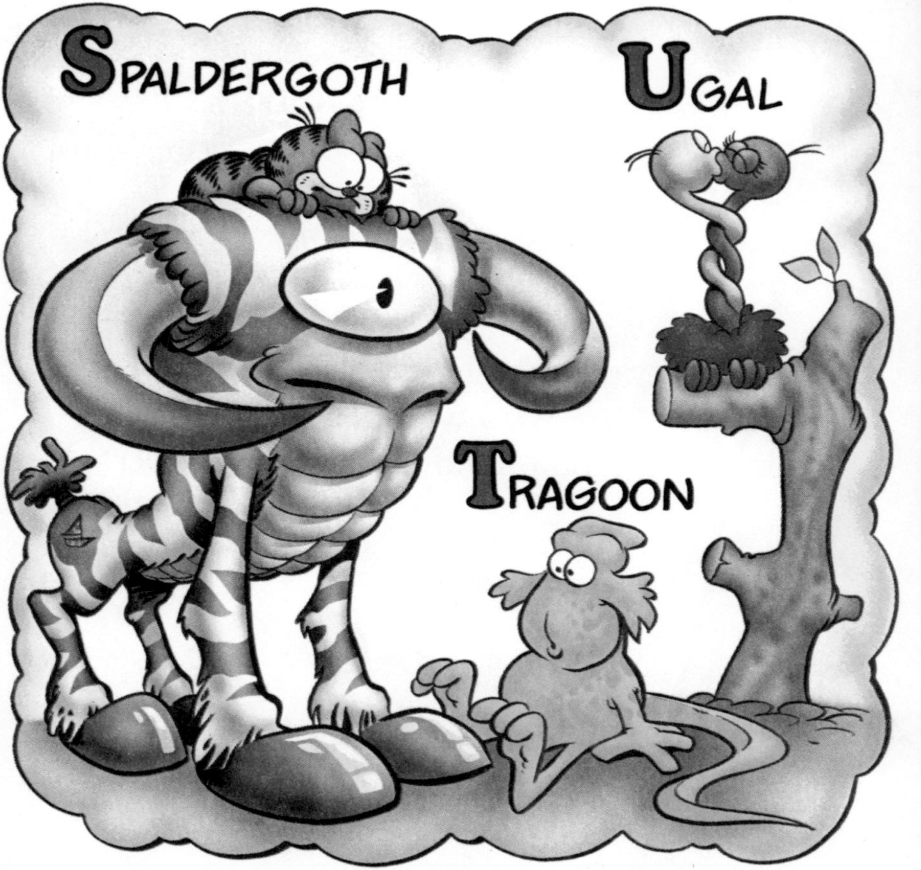
SPALDERGOTH
UGAL
TRAGOON

Vacuusaurus, who likes to tidy up the cage;
Wild Spamm, who watches too much
television; Xnail, who climbs skyscrapers;

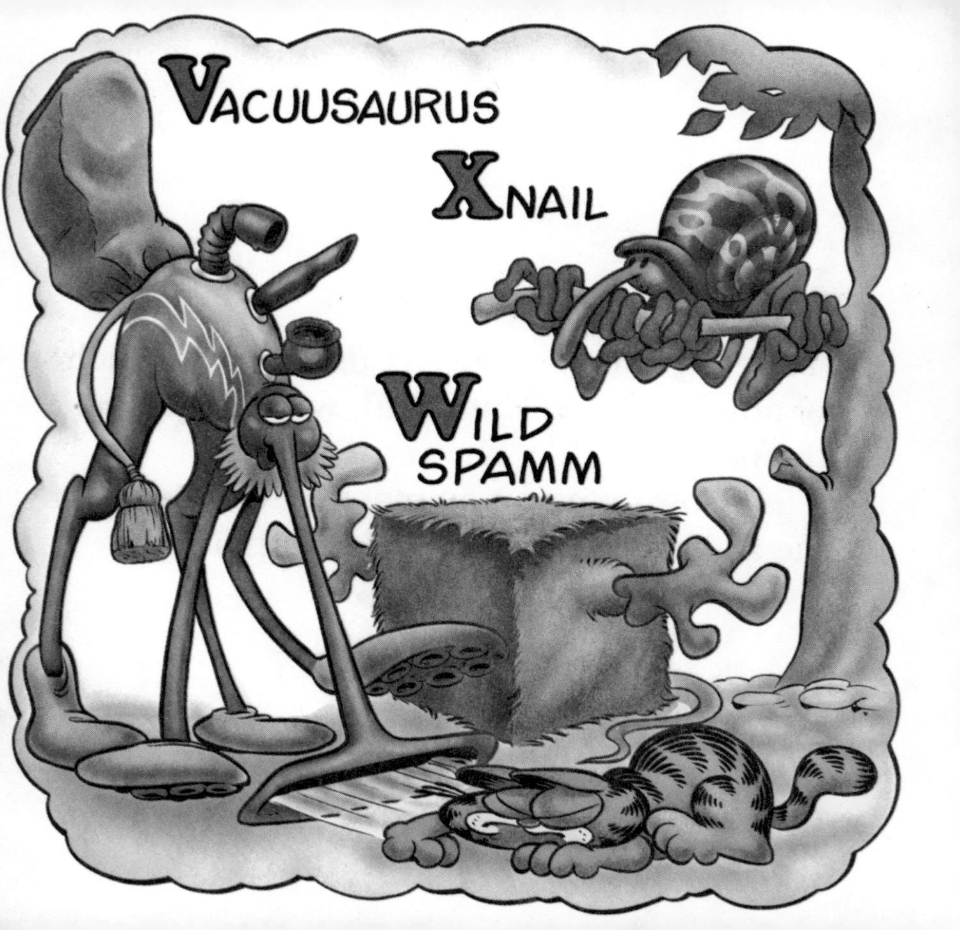
VACUUSAURUS
XNAIL
WILD
SPAMM

Yuhguk, who just doesn't understand much of anything; and Zuni Bird, who giggles on the phone.

Having found an animal for every letter of the alphabet, Garfield awoke with a start.

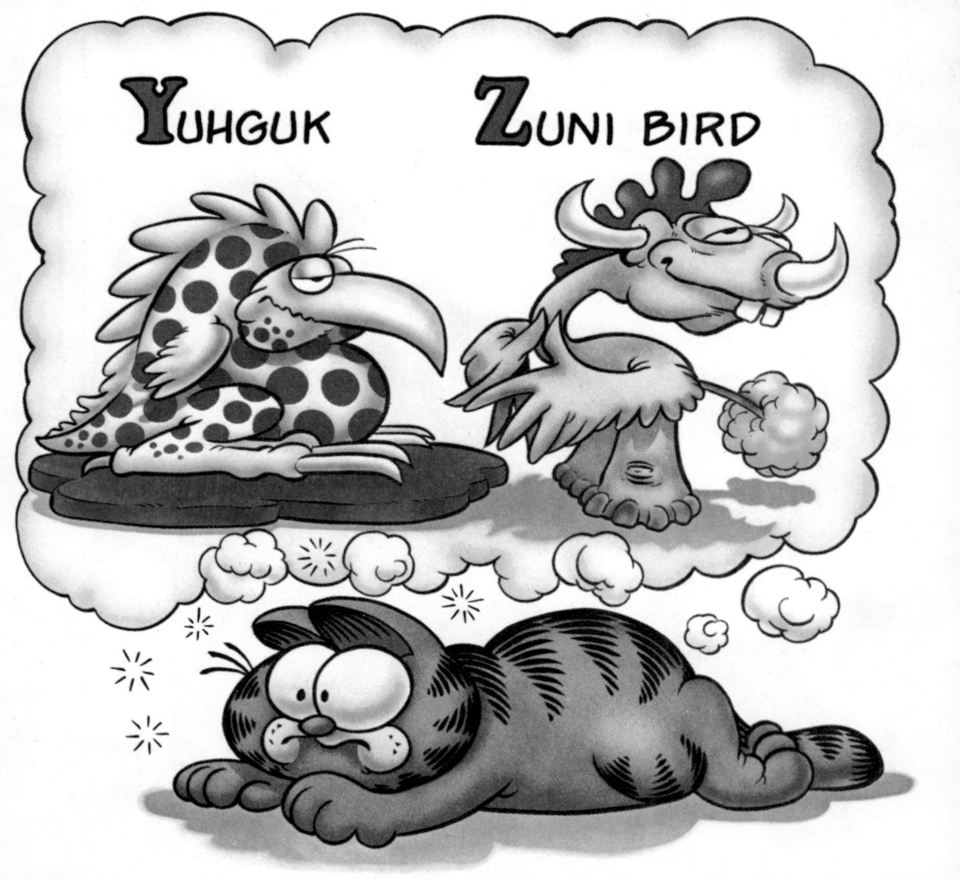
YUHGUK
ZUNI BIRD

Thinking he had seen the zoo, Garfield wandered home for a well-deserved nap.

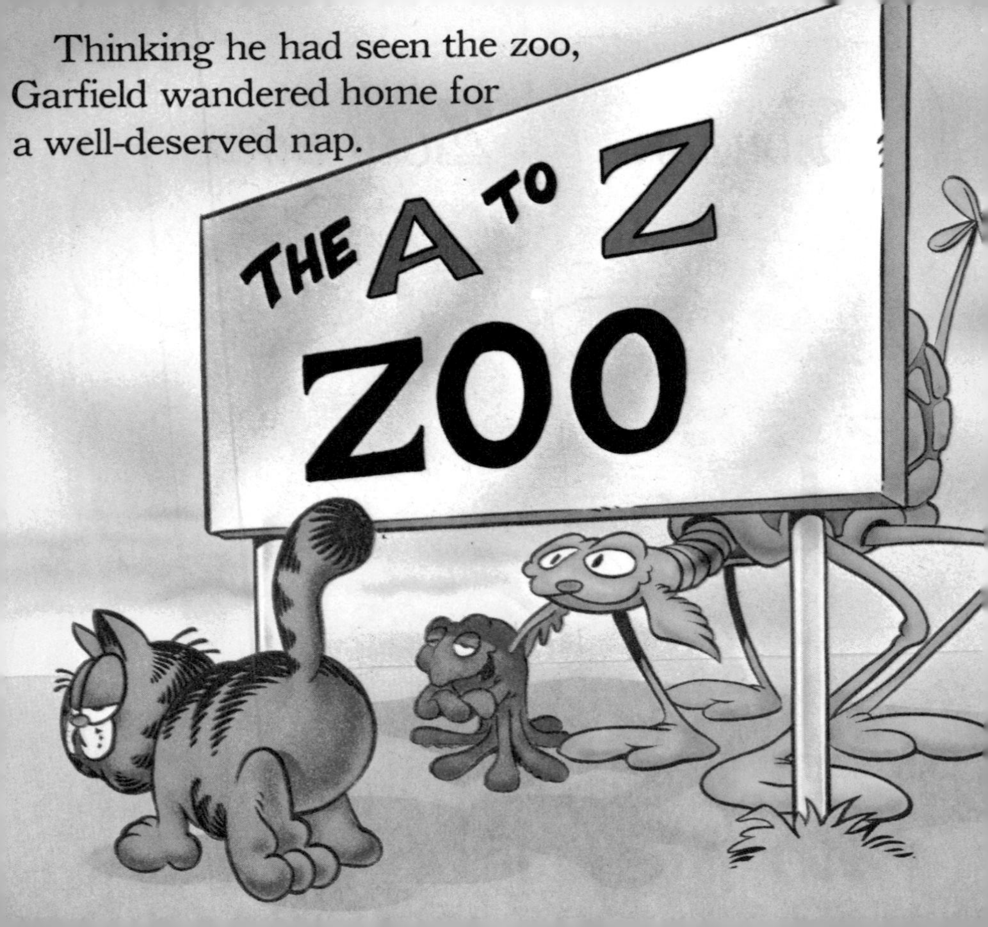
THE A TO Z
ZOO

The Mystery of the Sea Jellies

Written by Lisa Trumbauer

Illustrated by Julian Bruere

"Hey!" David called to his family. "I'm ready when you are!" He removed a hand from the handle of the towrope and shielded his eyes. His family's small powerboat drifted not far from him. David's father turned toward him, waved, and then began fiddling with the boat's controls. David could see his mother and his older sister, lounging movie-star fashion on the boat's benches.

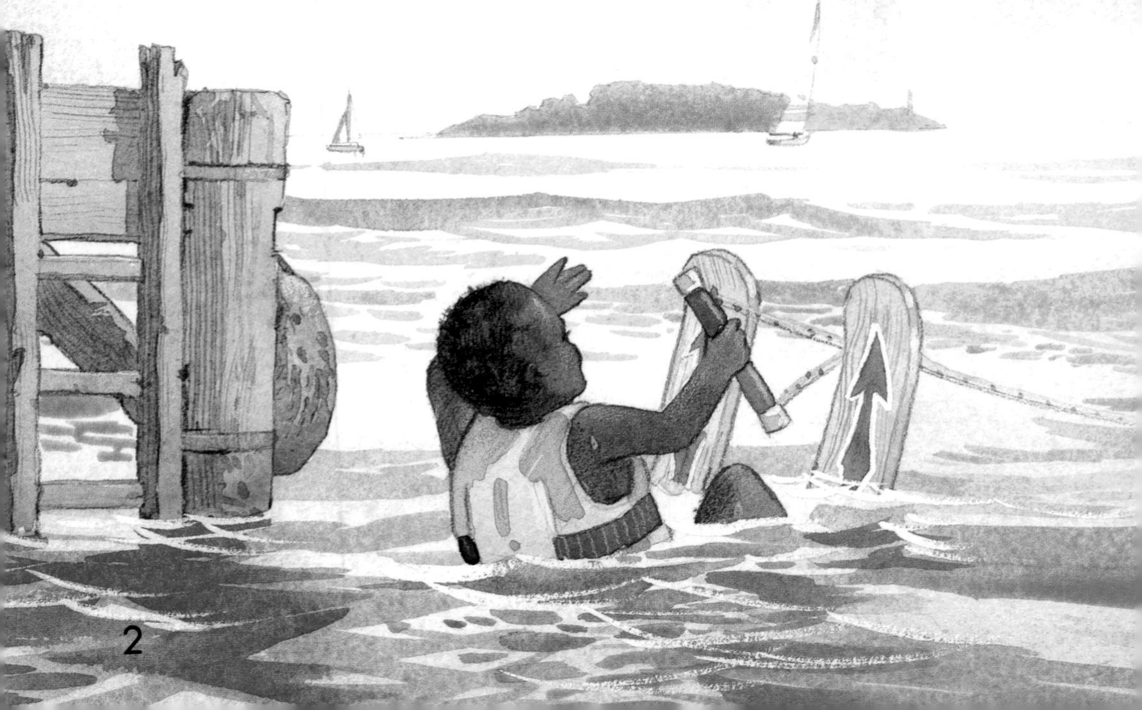

David bobbed in the water like a cork, grasping the handle in his hands. All around, the cool water of the Chesapeake Bay rolled gently. David rocked along with the rolls, his life vest keeping him afloat.

Then something brushed against his leg.

David jerked, and his skis wobbled from side to side. He whipped his head around, but he didn't see anything. Images of shark fins and sharp-toothed piranhas paraded through his head. He flailed about in the water. He didn't know whether he should float, extending his whole body across the surface, or kick off his skis, plunge his legs into the water, and begin kicking.

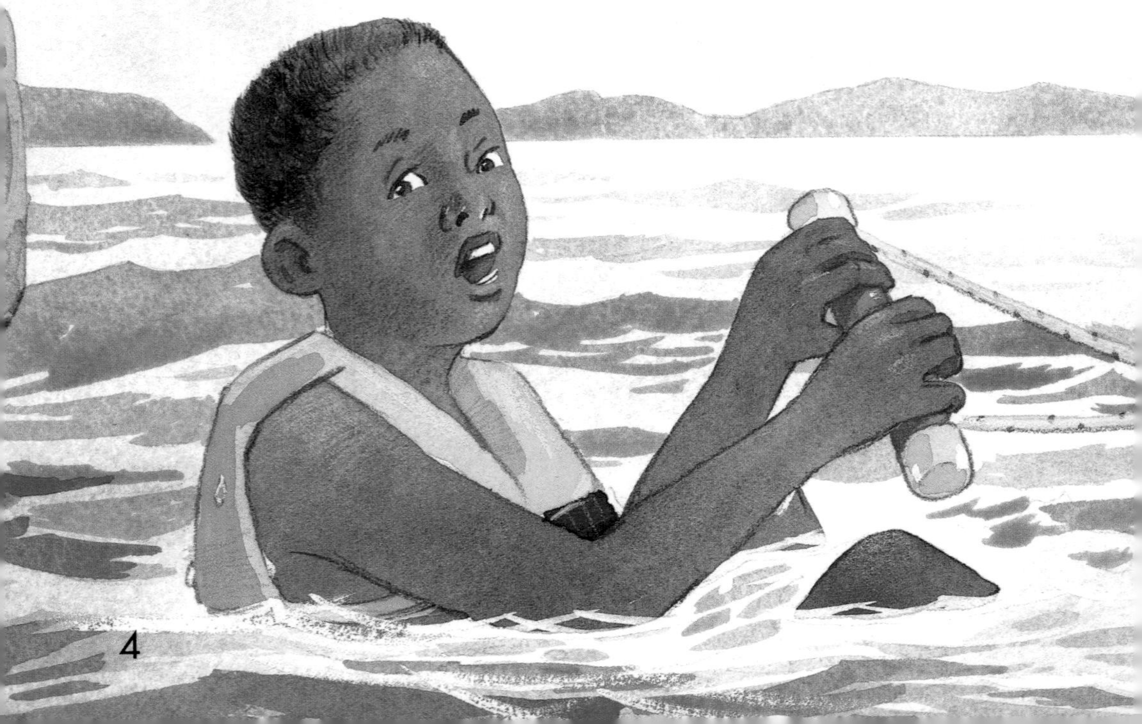

David gripped the handle of the towrope and prepared to be yanked forward. He watched as the towrope lifted from the water, and then became taut. Suddenly the boat's engine roared into life. He felt the pull as the boat began to drag him across the bay.

David's body rose quickly out of the water. It was then that David saw it. A huge white blob of a thing clung to his life jacket—a sea jelly. Its bulbous body was bell shaped, like a mushroom, and about the size of a grapefruit. Long, squiggly tentacles dangled from the bell-shaped body. Through its transparent, jellylike skin, David could see the muted colors of its insides.

As the boat pulled David up from the water, the sea jelly spread itself across the vinyl covering of his vest. Its tentacles dragged across his arm, leaving red welts in their path. Finally, David popped up on his skis, and the sea jelly slithered off into the bay.

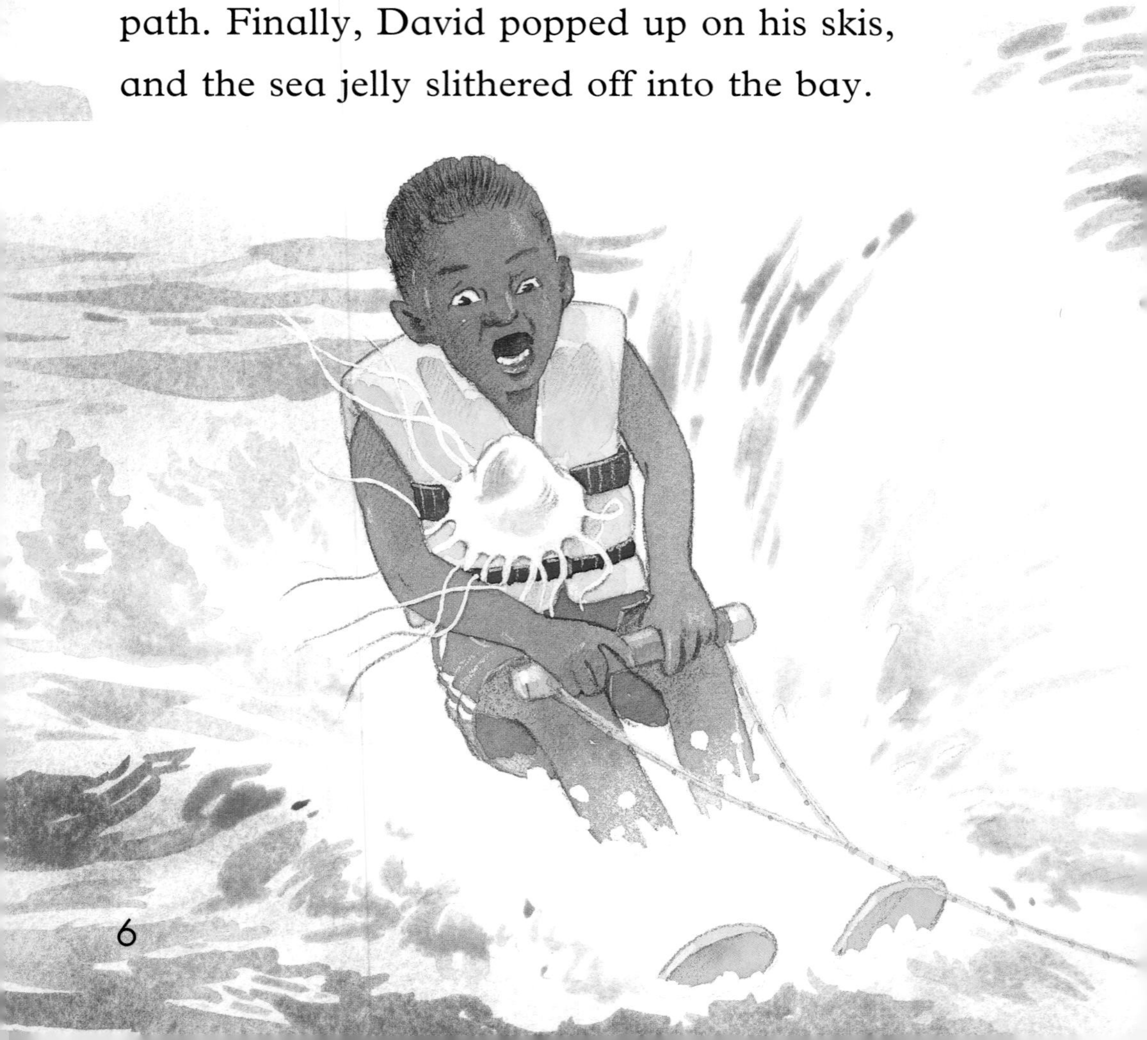

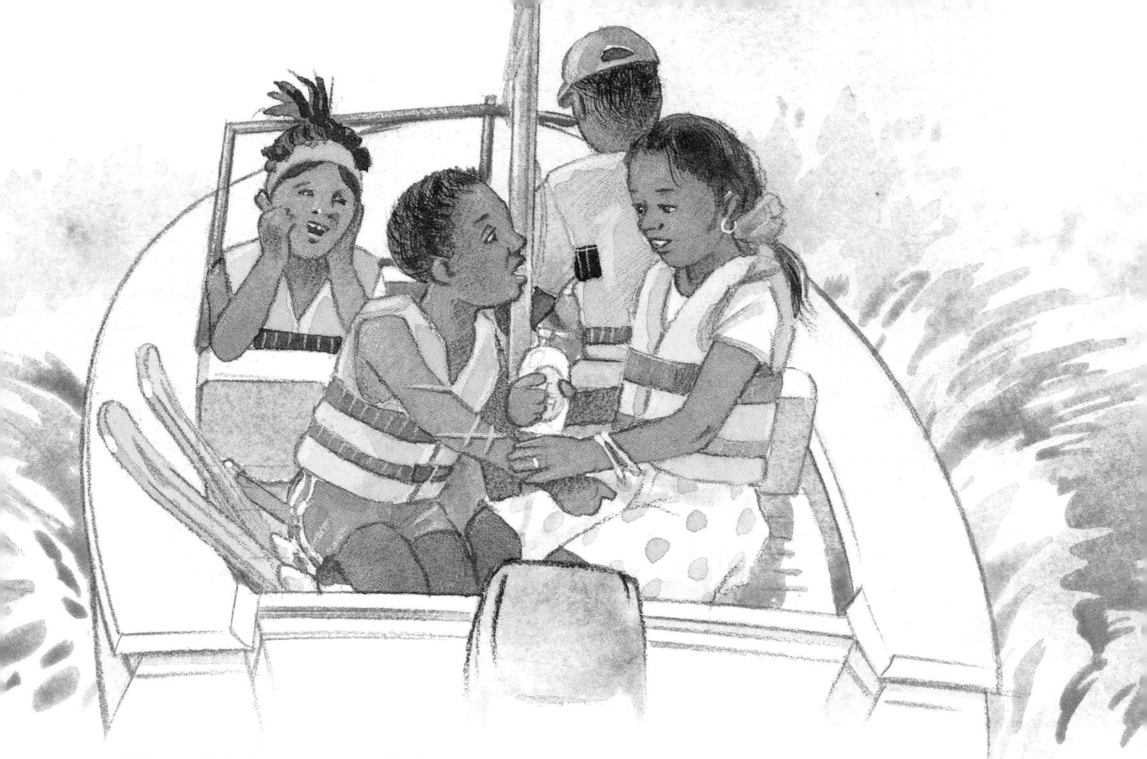

David let go of the rope and dropped into the water, and his dad circled the boat around to pick him up. David clambered into the boat. Painfully, he extended his arm toward his mom.

"Oh David, you poor thing," she cried. David winced as she spread lotion on his arm to soothe the sting. "That creature stung you pretty hard, didn't it?" she said.

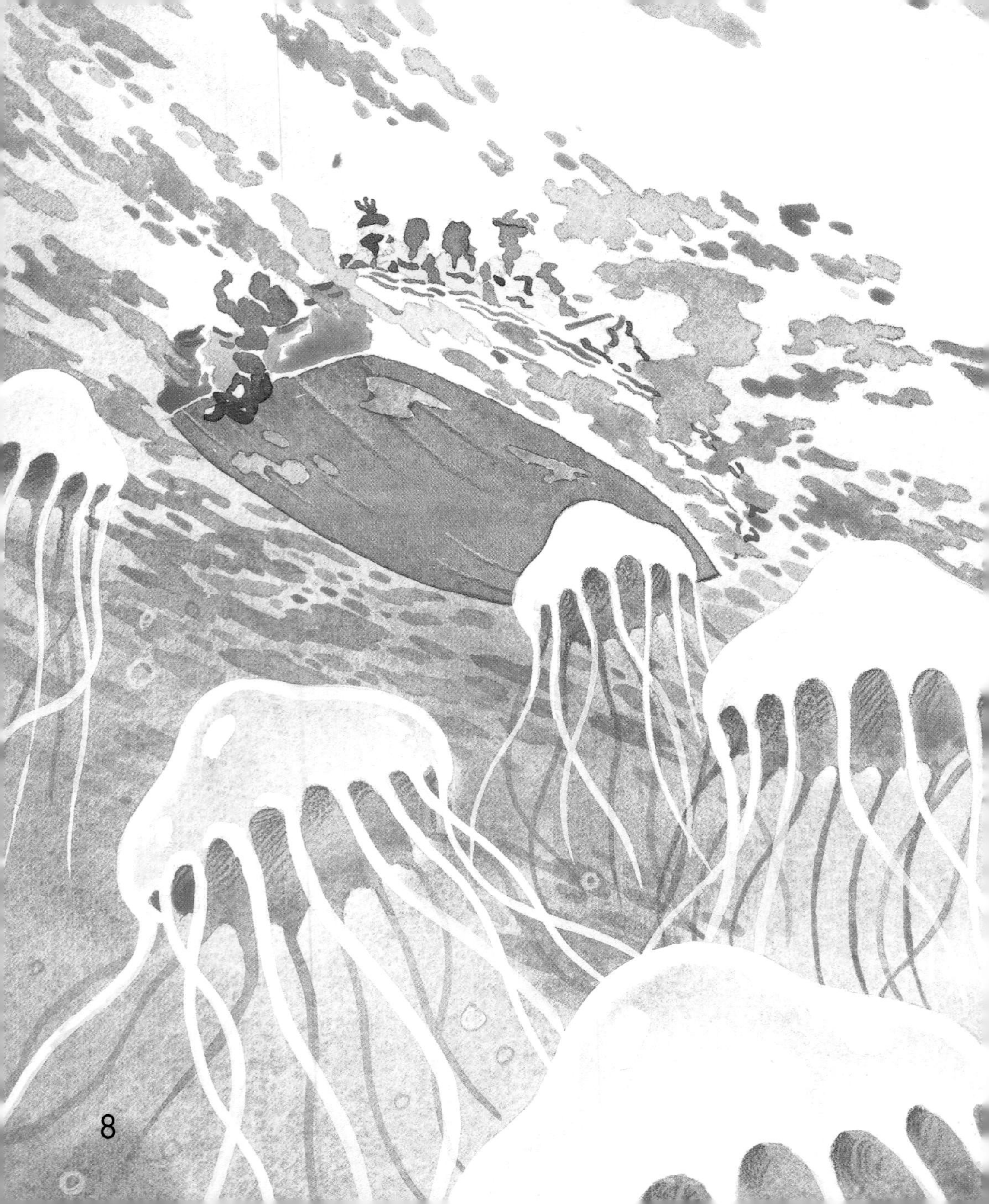

David peered over the side of the boat, watching a sea jelly bobbing along beside them, its dome ruffling in the waves. Its tentacles were stretched out behind it, like streamers on a wind sock. A few more sea jellies floated lazily nearby.

"Why are there so many jellies?" David asked.

"Who cares?" his sister, Katie, said. "As long as you don't go in the water, they won't hurt you." She shrugged indifferently and leaned back in the seat to absorb the sun's warm rays.

"Why should we have to stop swimming because of a bunch of sea jellies?" he asked. "I don't understand why they don't just get rid of these awful things."

Back at the quaint bed-and-breakfast where David's family vacationed every summer, they found Mr. Hutchinson, the owner, sitting on the porch.

"Ran into a sea jelly," David's dad said, pointing to David's arm as they trudged up the wooden steps.

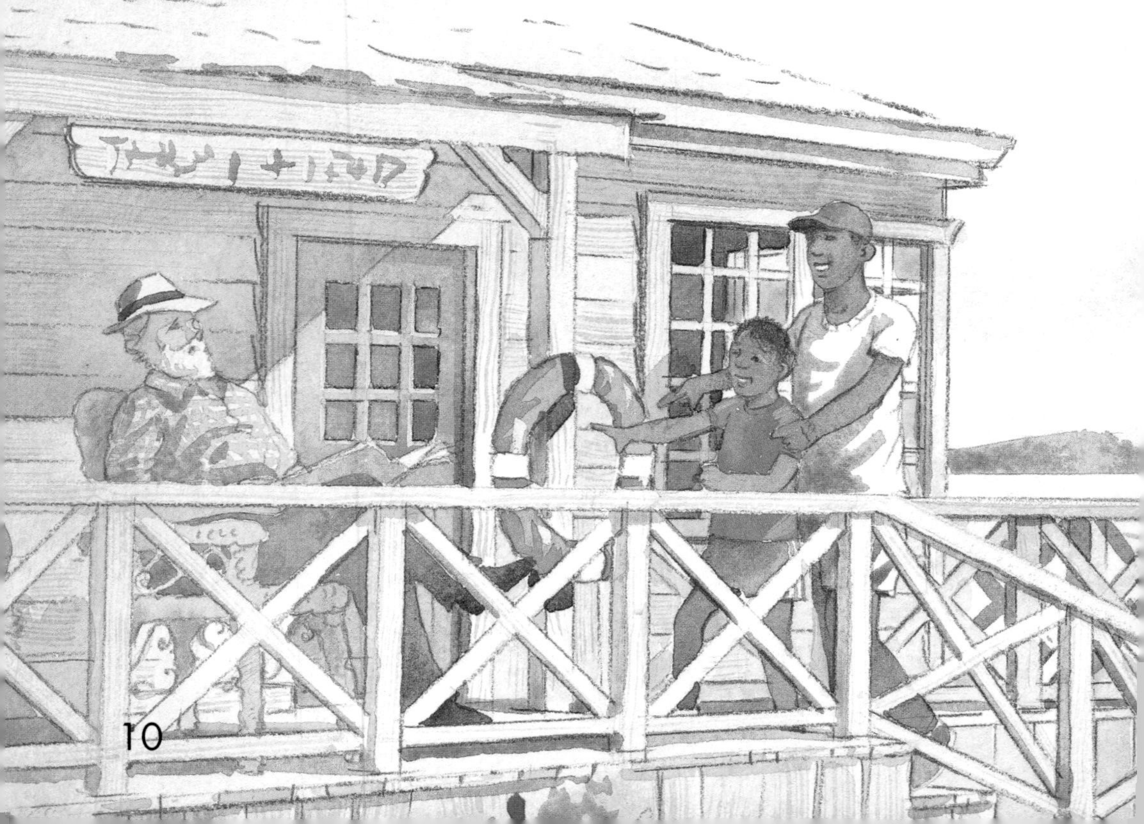

"All the summers we've been coming here, he's never been stung once," said David's mom.

Mr. Hutchinson scratched his chin. "Yes, well, usually you come in June. The sea jellies aren't out in full force until about August. Didn't you notice that not many people were in the water?"

"Why don't you get rid of them?" asked David.

Mr. Hutchinson chuckled. "Don't let the scientists hear you say that."

"What scientists?" asked David.

Mr. Hutchinson pointed. "Down by the pier. They come every year—just to study the sea jellies."

"They do?" David asked. "But why?"

"It's a mystery to me. You'll have to ask them that!"

David raced down to the water's edge. He slowed as he reached the wooden planks of the pier, suddenly not sure what to do. Several people squatted at the end of the pier, dangling devices into the water. Their heads were bowed together as they conferred quietly, jotting things down on their clipboards.

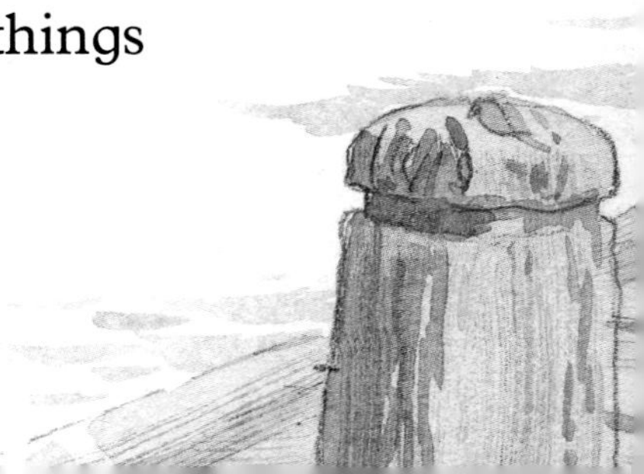

"Looking for someone?" said a voice behind David.

David turned. Standing behind him was a girl about his age, looking curious. "Well?" she said. "Are you looking for someone?"

"Actually, I'm looking for the people studying the sea jellies."

"That would be me," the girl said, placing her hands on her hips.

13

David narrowed his eyes. "I'm looking for a scientist."

Slowly the girl smiled. "Well," she said, "how about a scientist-in-training?"

David laughed. "I'll buy that," he said. "So tell me, how can we get rid of sea jellies?"

The girl's smile faded. "Get rid of them?"

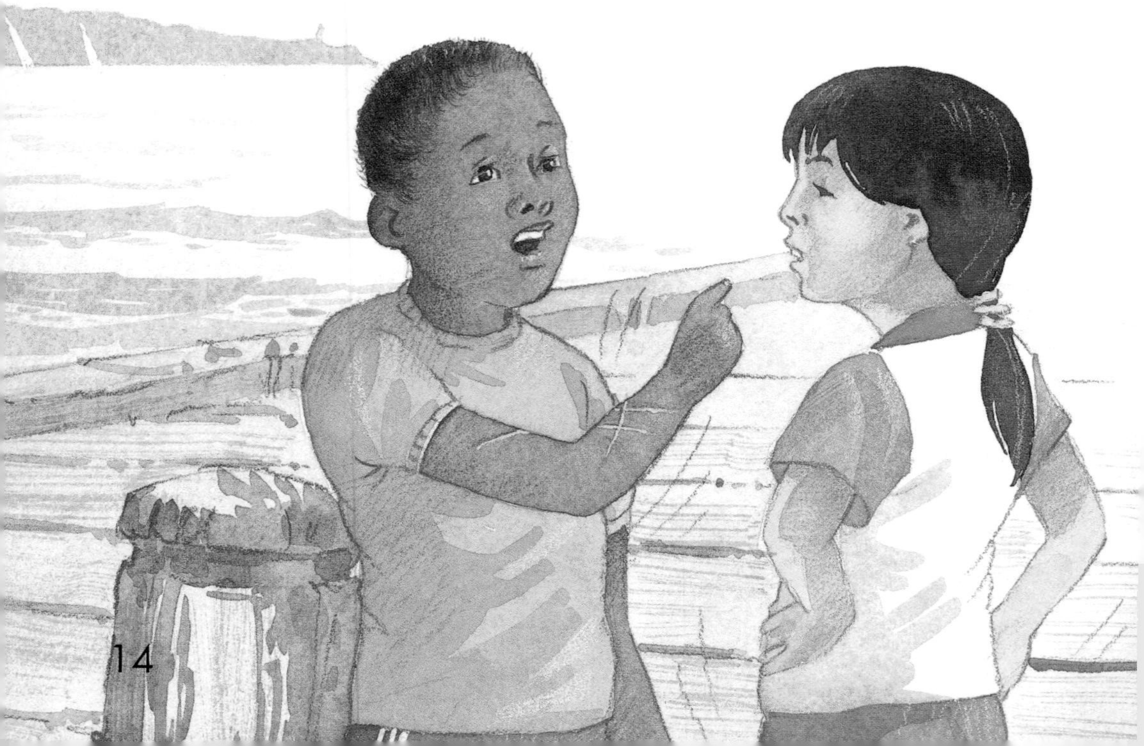

"Yeah." David extended his arm. "See this? This happened today when I was water-skiing. I think someone should do something so the sea jellies don't fill up the water and hurt people."

The girl leaned forward to look at David's arm. "Nice work," she said as a large grin spread from from ear to ear.

"It's not funny," David replied angrily. "It really hurt!"

The girl stopped smiling and tilted her head quizzically at David. "My name's Claudia Chu," she said. "What's yours?"

"I'm David. I'm from Pennsylvania," David replied.

"OK, David from Pennsylvania," she said, "let me take you to meet my mom and dad."

"This is David," Claudia said to her parents. "He wants to know how we can get rid of the sea jellies."

"David," said Mrs. Chu seriously, "Why would you want to get rid of the sea jellies?"

Claudia lifted David's arm for them to see. The sting marks had faded, but they were still visible.

"Ah." Mrs. Chu's voice softened. "You got in the way of one, didn't you?"

"I got in the way?" David asked indignantly.

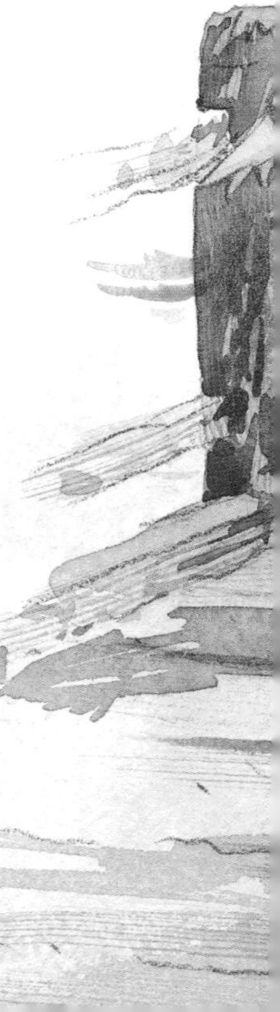

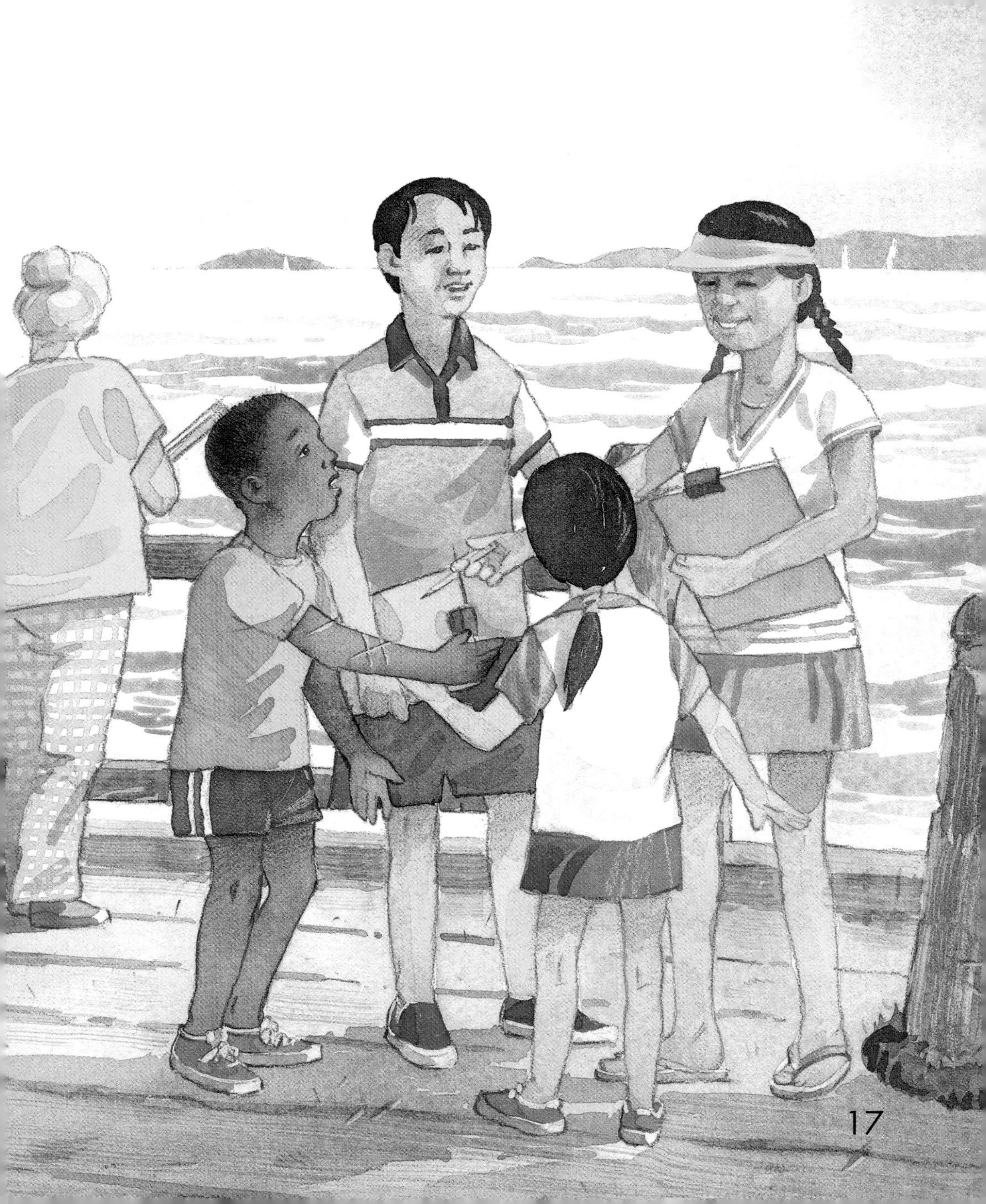

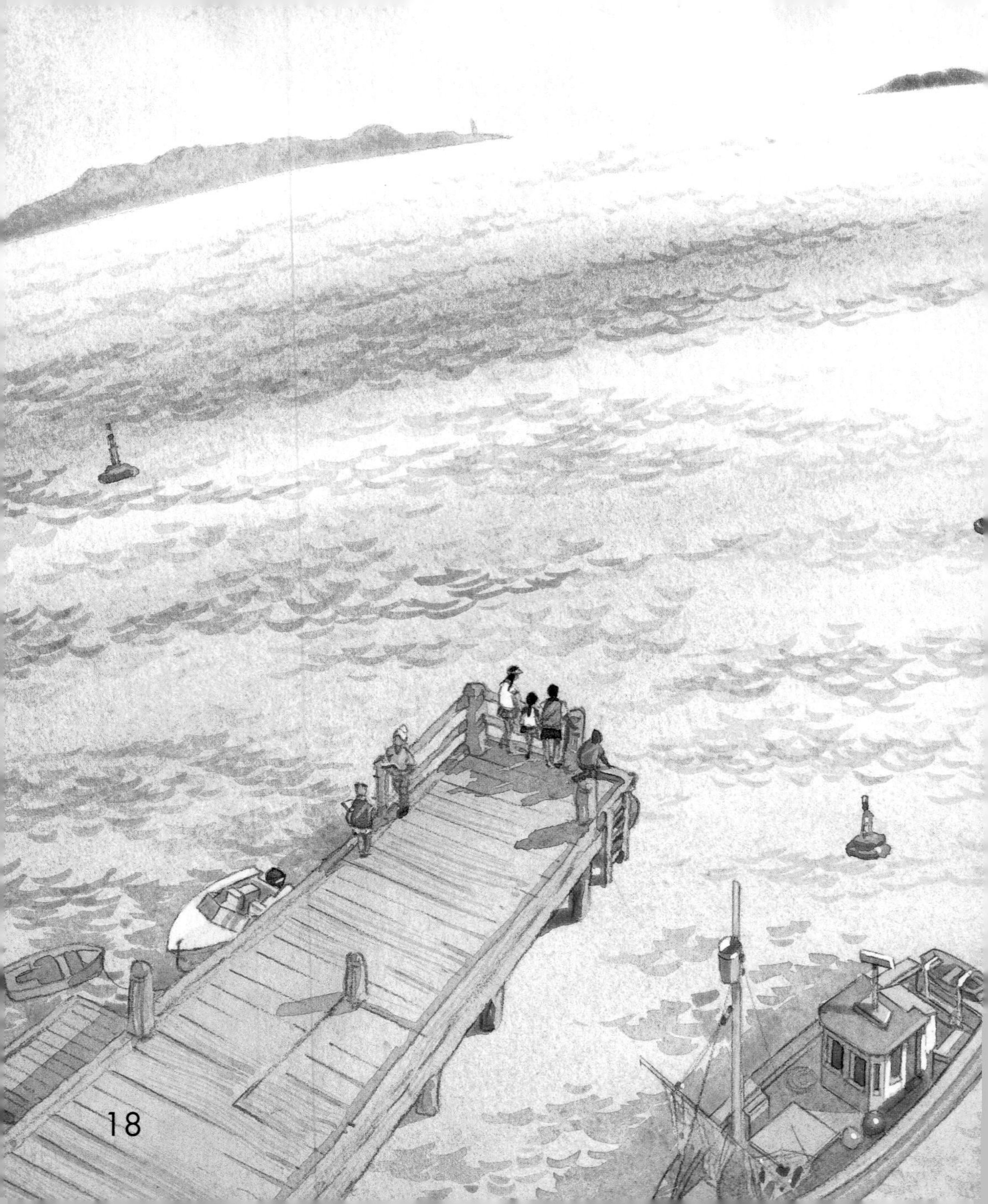

"Sure," said Claudia. "You were in the sea jellies' home."

"Their home? I was in the bay!" David clarified.

"Well," said Mrs. Chu, putting a hand on David's shoulder, "the bay is the natural habitat of these sea jellies."

"So?" David said.

She pointed to the water beyond the pier. "The Chesapeake Bay is a natural habitat, and although we might think it belongs to us, it really belongs to the animals that live in it."

"So, other animals live in the bay," David said. "What's the big deal?"

"These sea jellies, called sea nettles, are one small part of a bigger ecosystem," Claudia recited, as if they were lines memorized from a play.

"The sea nettles reach adulthood this time every summer. That's why you see so many of them," said Mr. Chu. "The adult sea nettles feed on very small creatures in the bay, like zooplankton, so they're important for maintaining the balance of life in the bay during the summer."

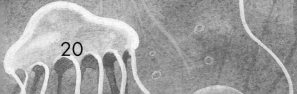

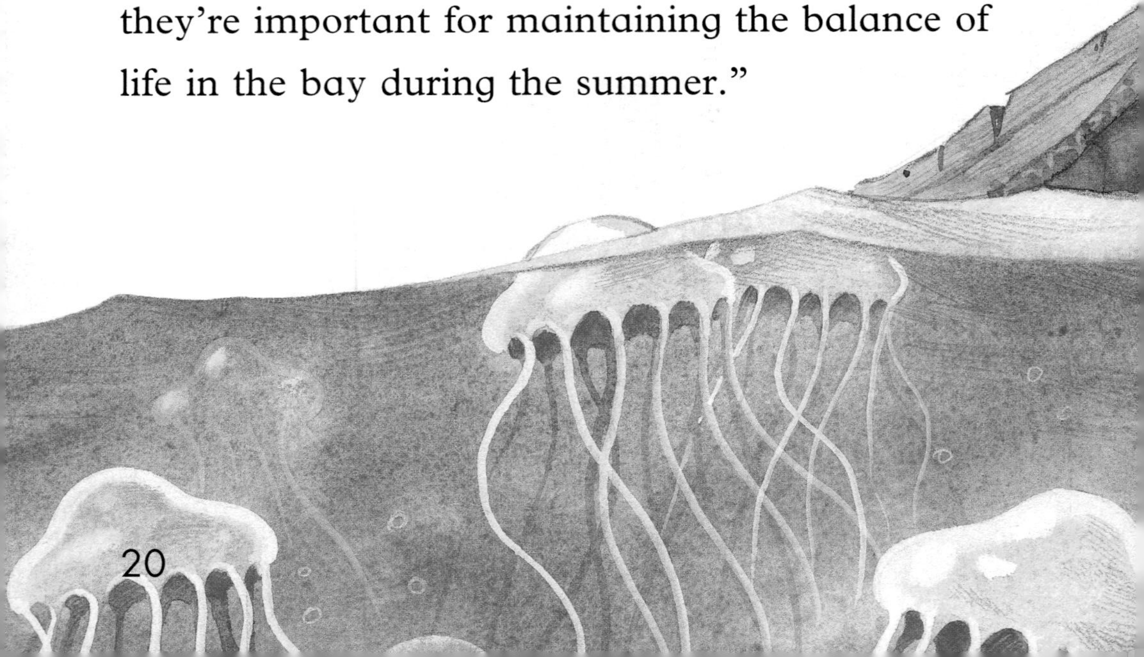

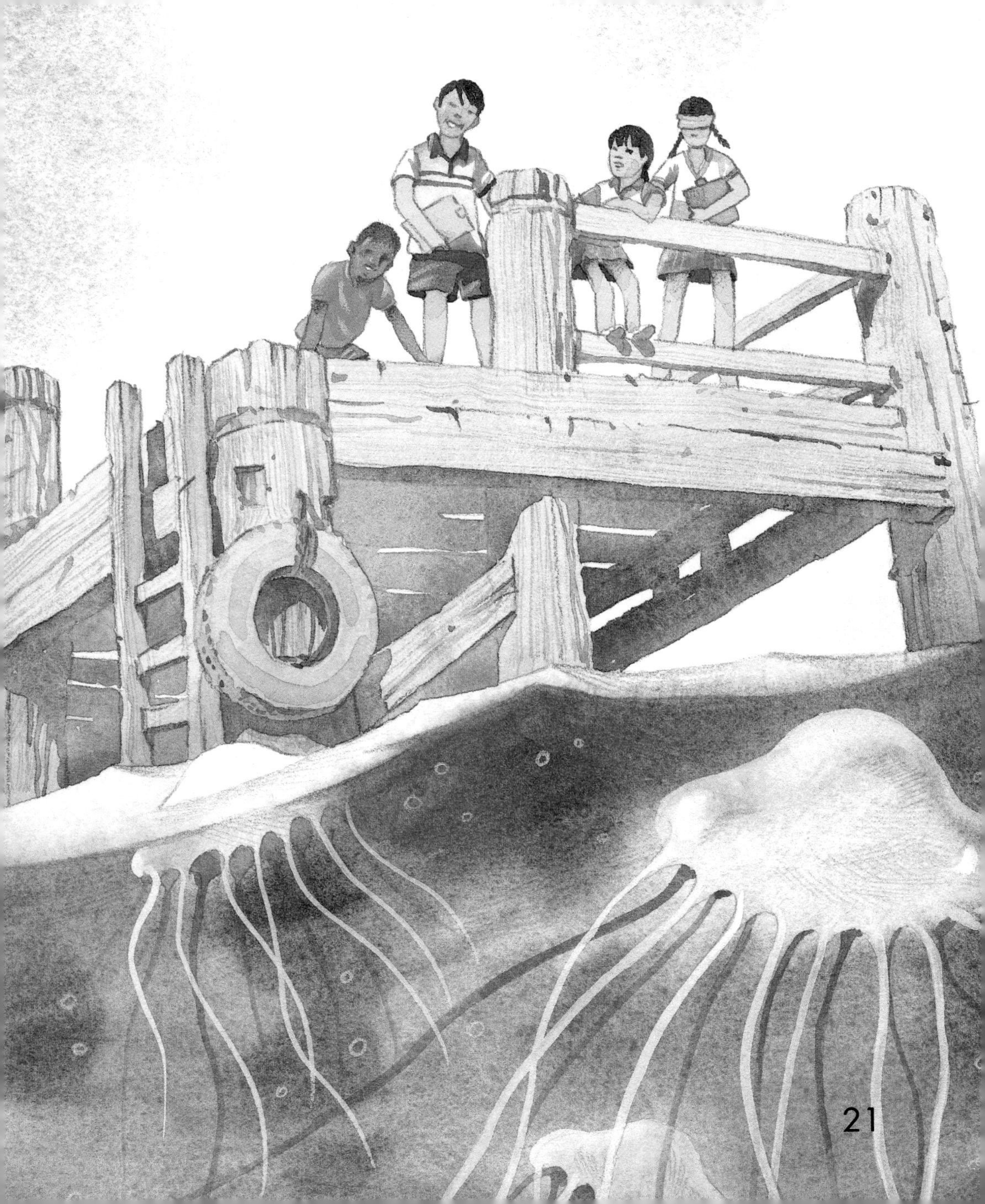

Then Mr. Chu asked David a strange question. "David, do you like to eat oysters?"

"I love oysters," David said, "especially with loads of hot sauce."

Mr. Chu laughed. "Well, you have the sea nettles to thank for the oysters you enjoy."

David wrinkled his forehead. "How's that?"

"We're studying the number of oyster larvae in the bay. Sea animals similar to sea jellies, called comb jellies, eat the oyster larvae," Mr. Chu said.

Claudia piped up, "And sea nettles eat comb jellies."

"So when the sea nettles eat the comb jellies, the oyster larvae don't get eaten," Mr. Chu added. "Then the oyster larvae have a chance to grow and develop into oysters."

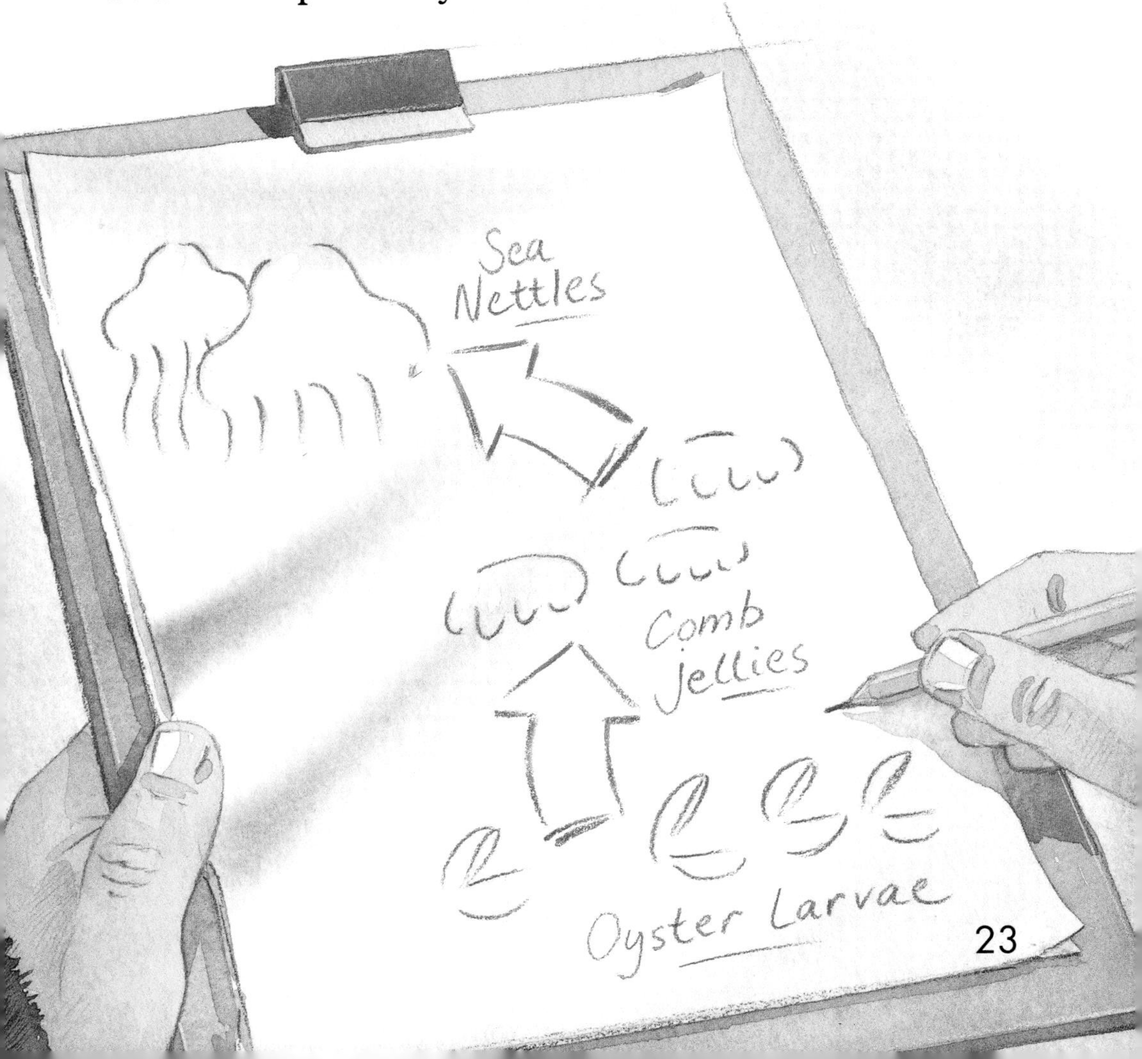

Sea Nettles
Comb Jellies
Oyster Larvae

David thought for a moment. "So I guess I shouldn't water-ski when the sea jellies are around, huh?"

"You can if you don't mind sharing the bay or getting stung!" Claudia said with a nudge.

David smiled and nudged her back. Now he understood why the sea jellies filled the bay and why it was important to study them. The mystery of the sea jellies had been solved.